TABLE OF CONTENTS

STARTUPS

PRODUCTS & SERVICES

BUSINESS OPERATIONS

SALES & MARKETING

HUMAN RESOURCES

CORE STRATEGY & PLANNING

ACKNOWLEDGEMENTS

This book is inspired by many people. Thanks are due to the business thinkers, management scientists and innovators who have researched, reflected, discovered and developed the frameworks that are explained in this book. Each framework has been illustrated in a simple and easy manner along with steps to use the framework and the typical use cases to make it easy for the reader. The tools and frameworks help the reader take the first step in pursuit of a solution.

"The Journey Of A Thousand Miles Begins With One Step – Lao Tzu"

Business is a progressive and practical enterprise and this book is designed to support the aspiring student, the entrepreneur and the career professional with great ideas. Business and management thinkers provide us with tools for structured thinking and problem solving and using these tools provide us with better outcomes for us and for our organizations.

Finally, I also would like thank my parents and my family for their unflinching support while writing this book. I hope this book helps you solving the problems at work but also helps you think through in new and different dimensions about business problems and the solution you can derive.

Anand Kumar

WHAT IS A GOOD APPROACH TO FOLLOW IN THE STARTUP PHASE?

Effectuation is an approach to making decisions and performing actions in entrepreneurship processes, where you assess the resources you have available and the derive the objectives you want to meet. It can be used to answer questions which start up founders have including : What do I do?, How do I get right talent?, What if I fail? and helps assess the objectives you want to reach realistically.

Effectuation Framework
Saras Sarasvathy

Overview

Effectuation is an idea with a sense of purpose and a thinking approach that serves entrepreneurs (novice and experienced) well during the startup phase of the business. It provides a way to control a future that is inherently unpredictable.

Key Steps

Step 1: Bird in Hand Principle – Start with your means. Start taking action, based on what you have readily available: who you are, what you know, and who you know.

Step 2 : Affordable Loss Principle – Set affordable loss . Evaluate opportunities based on whether the downside is acceptable, rather than on the attractiveness of the predicted upside.

Step 3 : Lemonade Principle – Leverage contingencies. Embrace surprises that arise from uncertain situations, remaining flexible rather than tethered to existing goals.

Step 4 : Crazy-Quilt Principle – Form partnerships. Form partnerships with people and organizations willing to make a real commitment to jointly creating the future.

Step 5 : Pilot-in-the-Plane Principle- Learn to Navigate. Knowing the market or predicting it is very difficult but learning to adapt and manage is critical for success.

Typical Use Cases

- Problem Solving
- Decision Making
- Business Planning
- Business Modeling

5

I HAVE AN IDEA, WHERE DO I START?

The Seven Domains Model helps you explore the impact of seven key domains on your planned venture or project and helps you analyse viability and feasibility of the venture or project.

Overview

This is a framework used for launching a new idea or a new project and helps test the idea from various perspectives including skills and attitude of the resources working on the idea as well.

Seven Domains Model

Mullins

Key Steps

Analyze your organization using the seven steps below and plan forward

Step 1 - Connectedness of value chain (Up/Down)

Step 2 - Industry Attractiveness/Market Attractiveness

Step 3 - Ability to execute on critical success factors

Step 4 - Benefits & attractiveness of the idea

Step 5 - Target segment

Step 6 - Does it provide sustainable advantage ?

Step 7 - Aligns with mission/aspirations and propensity to take risk ?

Typical Use Cases

- Business Strategy Planning
- Product Launch Strategy
- Operations Planning

HOW DO I BUILD A STRATEGY FOR MY BUSINESS? WHERE DO I START?

If your organization states that their strategy is to "increase revenue" or "become a global player" or "grow big" then strategy diamond framework is a tool which will help you understand the nuances of strategy and build a meaningful strategic approach.

Overview

This framework identifies five elements that makes up a strategy: Arenas, Vehicles, Differentiators, Staging, and Economic logic and states that it is essential that the five elements form a unified whole and reinforce each other

Strategy Diamond
Donald Hambrick – James Fredrickson

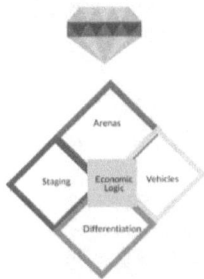

Key Steps

- **Arenas** - Where will we be active? which product categories, channels, market segments etc.
- **Vehicles** - How will we get there? Do we explore joint ventures, licensing, partnerships, franchising ?
- **Differentiators** - How will we win in the marketplace? Do we compete on price, quality, superior customer service, first to market or ?
- **Sequencing** - What will be our speed and sequence of moves?what is our go to market plan ? what is our strategy road map ?
- **Economic logic** - How will we make our returns?How do we make our money ? what is our profitability model ?

Typical Use Cases

- Business Strategy
- Product Management Strategy
- Sales & Marketing Strategy
- Business Planning

The SOAR framework is a take-off from the SWOT analysis with a focus on the positives and opening up opportunities for your organization.

Overview

This framework is an extension of the SWOT framework, however it focused on the strengths of the organization and way forward and typically deals with Innovation type work and captures the Strengths, Opportunities, Aspirations, Results. SOAR analysis is recommended after SWOT.

SOAR Analysis

Jacqueline Stavros - Gina Hinrichs

Key Steps

Analyse your organization using the framework and review

Strengths
- What are our greatest strengths ?
- What is our core competence ?
- What are we really good at ?

Opportunities
- What are our best opportunities to leverage ?
- What presents itself as the best way to capitalize what we do ?

Aspirations
- What is our preferred future ?
- What do we want to known for into the future?

Results
- How do we measure results that let us know if we are there or not ?
- How do we measure path forward ?

Typical Use Cases

- Organizational Planning

- Business Planning

- Strategy Building

HOW DO I ENSURE THAT MY BUSINESS IS UNIQUE?

Typically, USPs are often extremely difficult to find and unearth and the challenge is that once your organization establishes a successful USP, competition will rush to copy it. The USP analysis is a framework which helps you define your USP (Unique Selling Proposition).

USP(Unique Selling Proposition) Analysis

Rosser Reeves

What is it ?

This framework is used to focus on your product elements that distinguishes your organization from competitors in the industry. Typically USP can be built on on product characteristics, price structure, placement strategy (location and distribution) or promotional strategy. Be extremely forward thinking on this.

Key Steps

Process of defining your USP

Step 1 : List the tacit and explicit criteria that customers use in your marketplace to make purchasing decisions. Talk to all stakeholders to identify this criteria.

Step 2 : Rank yourself and your competitor based on this criteria.

Step 3 : Compare as to which criteria you rank well against your competitor and build your USP from thereon.

Step 4 : Plan out how you will build and defend on your USP once the competition comes in.

Step 5 : Build a USP on criteria which customers care about and not on something where you are only different.

Typical Use Cases

- Business strategy
- Go To Market Strategy
- Product Marketing Strategy
- Sales and Marketing Planning

WHAT ARE THE KEY FACTORS I SHOULD BE WATCHING OUT FOR IN MY BUSINESS?

PESTLE Analysis helps you analyse the Political, Economic, Socio-Cultural, Technological, Legal and Environmental changes in your business environment. This helps you to understand what critical changes are happening which could either be leveraged or watched closely as you move your business forward.

Overview

PESTEL is a framework used to analyse and monitor the macro factors that may have a profound impact on an organisation. This tool is especially useful when starting a new business or entering a foreign market and helps to give a clear understanding of industry and associated factors.

Key Steps

P - Political: All the influences that a government has on your business.
E - Economic : All the economic factors including economic growth, exchange rates, inflation rates, interest rates, disposable income of consumers and unemployment rates.
S - Social & Cultural : Includes social and cultural trends such as the population growth rate, aging, income distribution, career attitudes, risk tolerance, health consciousness, lifestyle attitudes and cultural issues.
T - Technological : factors pertain to innovations in technology that may affect the operations of the industry your business operates in.
E - Environmental : ecological and environmental aspects which may impact your business.
L - Legal : legalities in order to trade successfully and ethically for your business.

PESTEL Analysis

Typical Use Cases

- Business Strategy
- Business Planning
- Project Reviews
- Operational Reviews

WHO ARE THE KEY STAKEHOLDERS IN THE MARKETPLACE?

Building the right marketing relationships could be key to helping build a successful business model. The Value Net model is a tool that helps your business move away from "lets compete" model to a "lets co-exist" model and achieve greater success by operating alongside, or even in association with, other organizations.

Overview

The Value Net is an alternative to the Five Forces model and recognizes the importance of complementors as well as competitor products. The model focuses on the four main groups that influence a company's marketing environment: Customers, Suppliers, Competitors and Complementors and helps understand symmetries between the different stakeholders.

Value Net Model

Adam Brandenburger and Barry Nalebuff

Key Steps

Map out these stakeholders and study interrelationships and impact

Customer	Supplier
Map out people who buy your product and analyze	Map out internal/external stakeholders who provide the resources you need to produce a saleable product

Competitor	Complementor
The people who take a share of the target market by offering a similar product	The people that provide a product that can be linked to your own product to makeboth offerings attractive to end customers

Typical Use Cases

- Product Strategy
- Business Strategy
- Sales & Marketing Strategy

HOW DO I TRACK WHERE MY BUSINESS IS GOING?

You have to implement a project throughout the organization, you are concerned with how to steer everyone in the right direction and towards meeting the objectives of the project. Hoshin process can help in steering everyone in the right direction.

Hoshin Process

Yoji Akao

Overview
This framework is a strategic planning tool and is a variant of Deming's PDCA. This is primarily used to track organizational objectives.

Key Steps

- Key Objective - Define what you want to improve

- Sub Goals - Establish sub goals to meet objective

- Communicate - Communicate the plan

- Systemize - Develop system to track goals

- Analyze - Analyze results and take corrective action

- Check & Iterate - Repeat the cycle

Typical Use Cases

- Business Planning
- Tracking key business objectives

HOW DO I BUILD A BRAND AND ENSURE LOYAL CUSTOMERS?

What comes to mind when you think of the TATA group? What about Apple or Sony? each of these businesses have created and sustained specific and emotional ideas around their brand, and these ideas resonate strongly with their customers. A successful brand identity reflects values and beliefs, and how people would like to see themselves. Clarity and meaning is critically important in a brand. The Brand Identity Prism model helps you understand what you need to do to build a brand identity.

Brand Identity Prism

Jean-Noël Kapferer

Overview

This framework can be used as a checklist for identifying strengths and weaknesses of your brand. It provides you with six key aspects that you need to think about when developing a brand identity.

Key Steps

Step 1 : Physique - Examine the physical characteristics and main purpose of the product which evokes certain images, feelings and ideas in consumers. What are those ?

Step 2 : Relationship - Examine the relationship between your customer and your brand.

Step 3 : Reflection - How do your customers see themselves when they want to associate with your brand

Step 4 : Self-Image- How do your customers see themselves inwardly.

Step 5 : Culture - What culture does your brand express or want to express ?

Step 6 : Personality - what personality do you want your brand to have ?

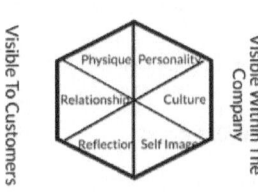

Typical Use Cases

- Product launch planning
- Marketing & strategy planning
- Business model building
- Branding & Profile Building

HOW DO I GET TO KNOW WHAT MY CUSTOMERS THINK ABOUT MY PRODUCT?

Empathy mapping is a framework which allows you to get closer to what your stakeholders really think and feel about your product, service or situation.

Overview

This is a framework to help get super close to your customer and to help observe what your customer sees, hears and does. It helps in better understanding your customer pain points, gain points and jobs to do.

Empathy Map
Dave Gray

Key Steps

- Identify the customer type
- Define scope of the empathy map
- Collect data using interviews, observation, shadowing etc
- Fill the template from a clockwise direction

Typical Use Cases

- Product Market Fit
- Customer segment identification
- Developing your Minimum Viable Product(MVP)
- Building business models

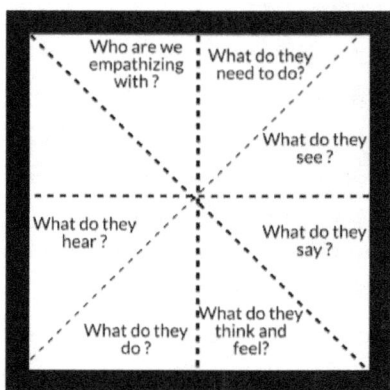

WHAT SHOULD BE THE PRICE OF MY PRODUCT?

Setting a price for your product is one of the most important factors that you will need to consider when bringing your product to market. If you set your price intelligently, you probably will generate good sales and high profits, however, set it too high or too low, and you risk losing both customers and revenue.

Overview

Pricing is one of the key levers used by CEO's to get their organizations leap frog ahead but getting it right is extremely difficult. Pricing is sensitive and companies are not always successful in implementing changes. Getting it wrong can be extremely costly.

Pricing Strategy

Cost Based Pricing

- What are the variable costs for the product you are pricing?
- What are the fixed costs for the company (rent, staff, utilities, infrastructure etc.), and how much of the fixed costs should be allocated to the product you are working on vs. other products?
- How many units of the product does the company expect to sell yearly?
- What margin do we want to achieve for the product?

Value Based Pricing

- What segment of the market are we planning to sell the product to ?
- What's the next best alternative to the product we are offering?
- What features make our product better than the next best alternative?
- How much are people willing to pay for these additional features?
- What is our USP ?

Competitor Based Pricing

- What other complementary p roducts can customers buy instead ?
- How much are our competitors charging for these products?
- Can we afford to price at the same level as our competitors?
- For how long can we sustain losses before key stakeholders question or we run out of resources?

Organizational Strategy Aligned Pricing

- What's the objective of our pricing strategy? Is it to win market share, increase profitability, etc.?
- Are there products we can cross-sell / upsell that we should consider when pricing this specific product ?
- Can we sell different versions of the product that differ in terms of quality, functionality, aesthetics, packaging, availability, or branding so that we can increase sales volume by appealing to more customers or increase profitability by selling at different price points ?
- Based on these strategic considerations, and the three approaches to pricing that we looked into, what should the price be?

Typical Use Cases

- Pricing Strategy
- Business Strategy
- Go To Market Planning

WILL MY PRODUCT SELL IN THE MARKET I HAVE IDENTIFIED?

Build Measure Learn loop gives you the opportunity to analyse how your customers use your product and allows you to develop your product through repeated iterative cycles until you have one that robustly meets the needs of your target market or help conclude that your product is failing to deliver its objective and course correct. Well suited for high risk idea validation.

Build-Measure-Learn Loop

Eric Ries

Overview

Build-Measure-Learn loop is a framework for establishing and continuously improving the effectiveness of new products, services and ideas quickly and cost-effectively and helps course correct in a timely manner.

Key Steps

Step 1 - Build

Identify problem to be solved (Hypothesis). Design the experiment, build the experiment, run the experiment.

Step 2 - Measure

Analyze the data obtained from the build phase and measure results against the hypothesis to check viability.

Step 3 - Learn

Learn from your results and either persevere(hypothesis is correct and you move on with same goals) or pivot(Refuted your hypothesis, reset, or correct your course and repeat the loop).

Typical Use Cases

- Idea Validation
- Business Model Validation
- Most suited for high risk, volatile environment idea validation

HOW DO I SELL MY PRODUCTS TO THE RIGHT CUSTOMER BASE?

How do you ensure that the savviest customers are targeted at the start of your product marketing effort? How do you match appropriate marketing messages to customers during a product's life? The Product Adoption Curve helps you predict customer behaviour so that you can target your marketing efforts intelligently.

Overview

This is a bell shaped curve which sheds perspective on how your product is adopted by customers in your market. You can build appropriate marketing messages for these customer groups to ensure product market fitment. 5 types of customers - Innovators(2.5%); Early Adopters(13.5%);Early Majority(34%); Late Majority(34%) and laggards (16%).

Product Adoption Curve
Joe M. Bohlen, George M. Beal and Everett M. Rogers

Key Steps

- Product positioning and marketing communication messaging must be appropriately tailored to ensure effective product adoption.
- Innovators will normally be the inquisitive type while the early adopters will be the discerning user, the early majority will look towards the early adopters and their opinions and reviews,while the late majority come in when product is mainstream and then the laggards adopt your product.

Typical Use Cases

- Marketing Planning & Strategy
- Product Planning & Strategy
- Business Planning

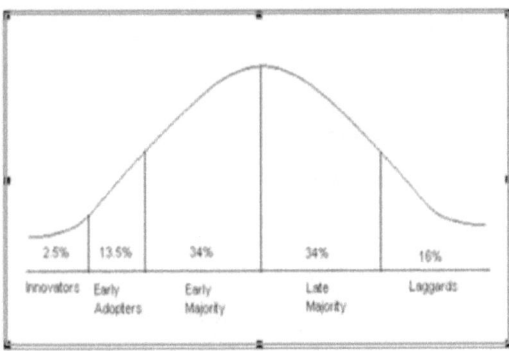

WHAT ARE MY CUSTOMERS THINKING ABOUT MY PRODUCT?

Perceptual mapping is a tool used to understand customer perceptions. How do your customers really feel about your product? do they think of it as utilitarian or pricey? how do they compare it with your competitor products?

Overview

This is a framework used to analyze how your target market perceives your product or service.They are also referred to as positioning maps and once you understand what your customer's perceptions are , you can work on building a sales and marketing strategy. Typically its a 2x2 map representing the dimensions you want to measure.

Perceptual Mapping

Key Steps

Use the steps outlined below in the context of your product or service.

Step 1 - Determine what you want to measure

Step 2 - Survey your customers

Step 3 - Plot the results

Step 4 - Analysis of the map

Typical Use Cases

• CRM Strategy

• Sales & Marketing Strategy

• Empathy Mapping

WHICH OF MY PRODUCTS IS DOING WELL, WHAT SHOULD BE MY FUTURE FOCUS?

If you have been asked to review your organization's products and decide which ones should be the focus for the coming year in terms of investment. Let's assume that one of your products is doing well financially but demand has fallen, and this trend looks set to continue. Let's also assume that another product is also doing well, but it is in a new market, and needs a lot of cash to support it. Should you continue investing in it? And another product is barely profitable, although its market is growing. Should you kill it or keep it? To make these decisions, you need to look beyond the income that the products are currently bringing in. You need to assess how they are going to perform in the future. This is where the BCG Matrix (aka growth share matrix or portfolio analysis) is extremely useful.

Overview

This framework helps organizations with the task of analyzing their products on two dimensions. The first dimension looks at the products in terms of growth within its market. The second dimension then measures the product's market share relative to the largest competitor in the industry.

Key Steps

- List your products
- Place products in grid
- Analyze the grid
- Decide future plans

Typical Use Cases

- Product Management Planning
- Market Landscaping
- Creating future business road map
- Building business models

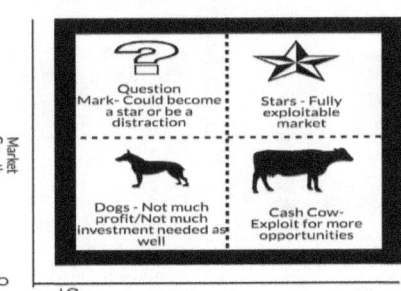

BCG Matrix

Bruce Henderson

WHAT DO I NEED TO KEEP IN MIND TO DELIVER A QUALITY PRODUCT?

Critical to Quality framework helps you understand what drives quality in the eyes of your customers, so that you can deliver a product or service that they are excited about. This also helps you stand out from your competition.

Critical To Quality Framework

Overview

This is a framework which helps translate broad customer needs into specific, actionable , measurable performance requirements. This in turn helps the business deliver superior products.

How To Use

Step 1

Identify Customer needs

Step 2

Identify quality drivers that need to be in place for product to meet critical customer needs

Step 3

Identify minimum performance requirements for your product to meet each quality driver

Step 4

Perform organizational assessment to determine capability to meet minimum performance and quality requirements

Typical Use Cases

• Product Strategy

• Business Planning

• Sales & Marketing Strategy

HOW DO I FIND OUT THE POTENTIAL MARKET SIZE FOR MY PRODUCT?

Analyzing your market size and using the data to make informed strategic decisions before launching your products is an effective way to ensure a successful launch of your product since product market fit is one of the key challenges for any organization and is typically a significant risk for start-ups.

Market Sizing

Overview

This is a tool used to understand total potential buyers of your product/service along with the potential revenue you may make. Typically used to identify Total Addressable Market (TAM), Serviceble Market (SAM) etc. It is also a guesstimate. There are typically top down and bottom up approaches. Bottom up is more tactical and is better in identifying target market and customer segment while top down could be used for pie-in-the-sky visioning purposes.

Key Steps

a. Identify if this is a demand side(combine end-user data with the number of operators within a market to create a formula that leads to the market size) problem or a supply side (estimate the market size based on the size of each competitor supplying the market) problem.
b. Demand side - Consumer segmentation, Occasions & Quantum of consumption for each segment, Frequency of purchase/replacement
c. Supply side -Volume/Value sales of each competitor, sales growth trend, Market saturation percentage? Are competitors providing the 'must-have needs' or 'good-to-have' or both ?
d. Form the mathematical equation with the variables
e. Calculate market size and do a reality check

Typical Use Cases

- Market size estimation
- Potential revenue estimation
- Product launch planning
- Marketing & strategy planning
- Business model building

HOW DO I MEASURE CUSTOMER SENTIMENT?

Net promoter score is a tool that measures the willingness of your customers to recommend your product or service to others. It is also typically used as a proxy for gauging your customer's overall satisfaction and loyalty to your product or service.

Net Promoter Score

Fred Reichheld

Overview

The Net Promoter Score(NPS) is a score that businesses get as the result of a user or customer survey that asks one question: How likely is it that you would recommend product X to a friend or colleague? It is measured on a 10-point scale that shows customer sentiment toward the vendor and the product in question.

Key Steps

- Ask the survey question and ask customers to rate you on a 10 point scale
- The results of the survey is grouped into three distinct categories.
- The first is **Promoters** – these are the survey respondents who answer the survey with a 9 or a 10 on the 10-point scale. They are seen as being positive enough about the company and its products or services to promote it to others.
- The second is **Passives**. Passives have scored the company a seven or eight on the 10 point scale. They are not really bending either way in terms of strong opinions and are passive customers.
- The third is **Detractors** Score , they have scored you in the negative range from 0 to 6. These are the people who may be at risk for churn and hence understanding their response will be critical.
- The NPS score is the difference between the percentage of Promoters and the percentage of Detractors and is as an absolute number between -100 and +100.

Typical Use Cases

- Customer Success Management
- Sales & Marketing Planning
- Highly used in B2B and SaaS Companies
- Sales and Marketing Strategy

WHAT IF I INCREASE THE PRICE OF MY PRODUCT? WILL DEMAND DO DOWN?

The price elasticity model is helpful when you need to explore the interplay between price and demand and understand the consequences of the same for your organization.

Price Elasticity

Alfred Marshall

Overview

This is a concept which helps you understand the extent to which the demand for your product is affected by the price you set and helps you analyze the interplay between change in demand and change in price.

Key Steps

Plot out the price vs quantity and analyze the data as you vary price and observe demand

1. Very important concept for determining product pricing models.
2. In some cases, demand will significantly vary based on price.
3. Some products have inelastic pricing, which means demand is constant irrespective of price.
4. Mapping price vs. quantity demanded allows businesses to predict changes in revenue based on changes in pricing.
5. Organizations can alter product pricing based on elasticity in income in different markets.

Typical Use Cases

- Pricing Strategy & Pricing Models
- Business Strategy
- Marketing Planning and Strategy
- Sales Strategy

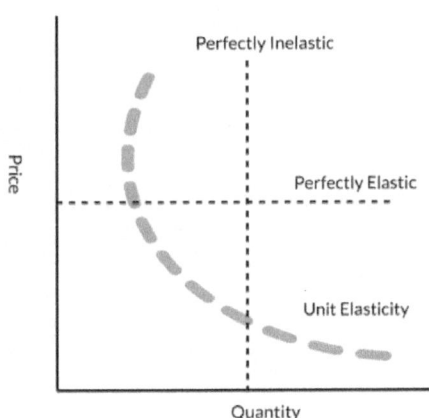

WHAT ARE KEY FINANCIALS TO KEEP IN MIND WHEN I AM RUNNING MY BUSINESS?

Analysing your company's operations and calculating the profitability of your business is a critical task and the margin and return ratios are a key indicator of the financial health of your organization.

Overview

Typically, analyzing profits can be done using Margin ratios and Return ratios. Margin ratios represent the company's ability to convert sales into profits (various degrees of measurement). Return ratios represent the organization's ability to generate returns to its shareholders.

Profitability Ratios

Margin Ratios

Gross Profit Margin- reveals the amount of money left over from sales after deducting the cost of goods sold. It is calculated by subtracting cost of goods sold (COGS) from total revenue and dividing that number by total revenue. A high number means the business is efficient

EBITDA - Earnings Before Interest, Taxes, Depreciation, and Amortization. It represents the profitability of a company before taking into account non-operating items like interest and taxes, as well as non-cash items like depreciation and amortization

Operating Profit Margin- analyzes earnings as a percentage of sales before interest expense and income taxes are deduced. High operating profits are good

Net Profit Margin- percentage of revenue left after all expenses have been deducted from sales. The measurement reveals the amount of **profit** that a business can extract from its total sales

Cash Flow Margin-It tells how well the company converts sales to cash. Calculated as cash flow from operational activities divided by sales

Return Ratios

Return On Assets - is the percentage of net earnings relative to the company's total assets. The ROA ratio specifically reveals how much after-tax profit a company generates for every one dollar of assets it holds. It also measures the asset intensity of a business

Return On Equity-the rate of return on the money that equity investors have put into the business. The ROE ratio is one that is particularly watched by stock analysts and investors

Return On Capital- is a measure of return generated by all providers of capital, including both bondholders and shareholders

Typical Use Cases

- Business Planning& Operations
- Profitability Assessment
- Financial Statement Preparation

WHAT ARE THE DIFFERENT PRICING MODELS FOR MY BUSINESS?

How do you find the competitive edge and meet customer needs better than any other company in an open market? How does your company gain competitive advantage over the others? And when there are only a finite number of unique products and services out there, how do different companies sell basically the same things at different prices and with different degrees of success? The strategy clock framework helps you think through those options.

Overview

This is a framework which could be used to understand how companies compete in the marketplace using different combinations of price vs, perceived value. In many instances, companies having potentially similar products compete using different combinations of value vis-a-vis price combinations.

Key Steps

Use the model to analyze where your company stands against your competitors and plan out future steps

Typical Use Cases

• Your Pricing Strategy
• Your Product Positioning
• Developing your marketing strategy
• Building business modes

Strategy Clock

Cliff Bowman and David Faulkner

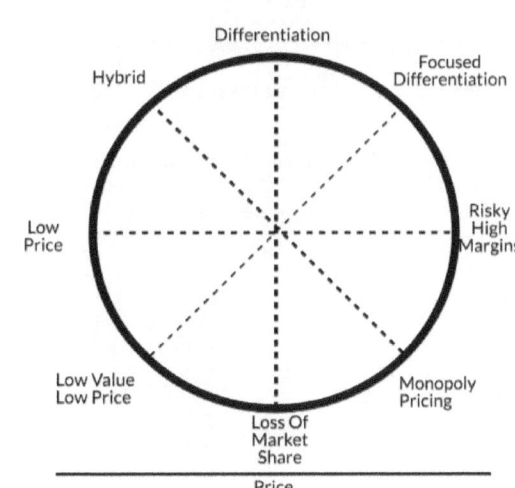

HOW DO I FIX MY CUSTOMER SUPPORT ISSUES?

Future state mapping is a framework which could help fix existing mistakes and plug existing service gaps(in case they exist) and help design and implement a completely new customer experience.

Overview

This framework helps in differentiating from competitors by helping redesign customer experiences with new ways of interaction by analyzing current state and defining future state. It can help answer questions like - "what does our future customer journey look like?" , " what does our future customer experience look like ?"

Future State Mapping

Key Steps

Step 1 - Form Stakeholder Group.

Step 2 - Map current state customer experience.

Step 3 - Define business goals and customers.

Step 4 - Brainstorm, generate new ideas, map future state.

Step 5 - Analyze and validate future state map.

Step 6 - Implement Future state map.

Typical Use Cases

- Ideation Exercise
- Future business planning
- Customer perspective mapping

WHAT ARE THE KEY ASPECTS ABOUT THE MARKET FOR MY PRODUCT?

If you need to develop a strategy for your organization, one of the first things you can explore is to look at using the 3C framework. This framework helps understand how to start to develop a strategy for your organization as it strips strategy down to its essentials.

3C (Customer, Corporation and Competitor) Framework

Kenichi Ohmae

Overview

This is a framework used for strategic analysis and identifying interlinkages between your customers, your corporation and your competitors. The analysis is frequently used for understanding the market landscape and for business planning and outperforming competition.

Key Steps

- Customer - Who is the customer (segment, trends in terms of customer data, % Market Share), What are the needs and wants of the customer segment?, What are the price points which each segment is willing to pay?, What are the natural partners and preferred distribution channels?, What is the threat from the buyer ?(buyer power)
- Corporation - Company reputation, Special barriers to entry (IP etc ?), Competence and capabilities analysis ?, Supply chain and distribution models ?, Cost structure , ROI expected , Branding
- Competitors- Market share,products,Supply chain strategy, branding, USP, Benchmarks established , Barriers to entry
- Complete analysis and draw inferences and plan ahead

Typical Use Cases

- Business strategy
- Go To Market Strategy
- Product Marketing Strategy
- Sales and Marketing Planning

MY PRODUCT IS GOOD BUT IT IS STRUGGLING TO SELL, WHAT DO I DO?

You have probably been in situations where you know how you want people to use your product, you have carried out interviews, surveys, community focus group meetings and you have heard about how people share that they use your product, yet your product seems to be struggling. Business ethnography is the use of direct observation and interviews to reveal your customers true behaviours and motivations.

Overview

This technique could be used to identify unmet customer needs, develop new products, devise marketing strategies and brand positioning. It is typically the analysis of
customer motivations/behavior in using your product/service.

Business Ethnography
Gerhard Friedrich Müller

Key Steps

- Define the Key Business Objective and reframe the problem.
- Collect data on how customers use your product
- Examine the data for patterns and trends
- Curate and create key insights
- Build business impact

Typical Use Cases

- Uncover customer persective
- Refine customer engagement models
- Develop new positioning and communication
  models

HOW DO I INCREASE MY PROFITS AND EXPLORE GETTING NEW CUSTOMERS?

If you have been asked to find ways to increase profits, you will need most likely need to find new ways to increase profits and reach new customers. The Ansoff matrix helps in identifying options.

Overview

This is a tool used by firms to analyze and plan their strategies for growth. The matrix shows four strategies that can be used to help a firm grow and also analyzes the risk associated with each strategy. It is also called the Product/Market expansion grid.

Key Steps

You need to decide which of the possible four strategies is more beneficial and potentially less risky for your business by planning your products vs. market.

Typical Use Cases

- Product Market Fit

- Customer segment identification

- Building business models

- Sales and Marketing Strategy plans

Ansoff Matrix

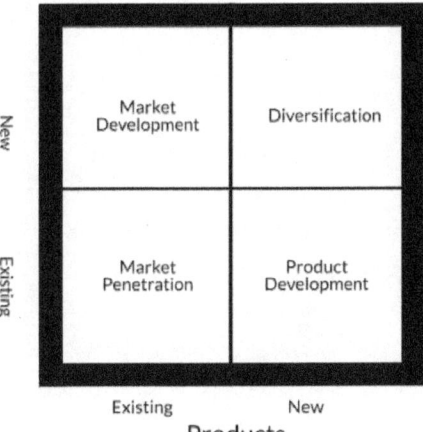

HOW IS MY BUSINESS DOING FROM A HOLISTIC PERSPECTIVE?

If you have been asked to explore ways to measure how the overall organization is performing and also have been tasked with figuring out a tool to track as well. Further, the CEO states that CFO measures financial progress but she needs to track how other functions are performing. The balanced score card is one way to do it as it helps measure non-financial aspects of an organization.

Balanced Scorecard(BSC)

Kaplan and Norton

Overview

The BSC is a framework to implement and manage organizational strategy by linking vision to strategic objectives, measures, targets, and initiatives. It balances financial measures with measures from other parts of the organization i.e. Learning and growth, internal business process, customer objectives and maeasures.

Key Steps

Step 1 : Identify your organization's strategic objective

(learning and growth, internal business processes,

customer, and financial).

Step 2 : Create a strategy map that shows the relationships

and interconnections between your different strategic

objectives.

Step 3 : Outline the specific metrics you will use to measure

success for each strategic objective. The key here is to list

out the measures for each objective and then outline the

current state metric and the future goal

Typical Use Cases

- Performance Management System
- Business goals tracking system
- Metric based business models

WHAT STEPS TO TAKE TO ENSURE TOTAL QUALITY IN MY BUSINESS?

When quality is something which needs to be maintained at high levels, TQM is a framework which helps you precisely do that. TQM is a management philosophy in which everyone in the organization strives to continuously improve customer satisfaction while maintaining emphasis on planned improvement that provides the best possible products and services.

Total Quality Management (TQM)
Joseph Juran

Overview

TQM is a management system for a customer-centric organization and typically uses strategy, data, and effective communications to integrate the quality discipline into the culture and activities of the organization. There are eight principles to this.

Key Steps

Principle 1 : The customer defines the quality and hence the organization should be customer focused.

Principle 2 : The effort towards TQM involves total employee commitment.

Principle 3 : Processes help deliver consistency

Principle 4 : TQM requires an integrated system which connects business improvement initiatives to continually improve and exceed the expectations of customers, employees, and other stakeholders.

Principle 5 : The Formulation of a strategic plan that integrates quality as a core component is important and delivers a strategic and systematic approach

Principle 6 : Continuous improvement is a key part of staying competitive and delivering quality

Principle 7 : Fact based decision making is critical for TQM

Principle 8 : Effective communication methods and timeliness is key for TQM

Typical Use Cases

- Quality Control
- Quality Assurance
- Quality based business models

FIXING MY BUSINESS CHALLENGE (NEW PRODUCT, PROFITABILITY, STRATEGY)

When your business is in a situation where it needs to review its core capabilities, assess competitors and determine the steps the business needs to take in the marketplace. This could be due to many reasons – business not doing well, or new product launch or growth planning or new business strategy launch.

Overview

This framework helps you when analyzing a new market entry approach or a new business approach or a growth strategy or a turnaround strategy or an organizational assessment by helping you identify key factors you need to keep in mind during the course of the initiative. Using Ansoff, Porters 5 forces, PESTEL, BCG will help.

Business Situation Analysis
Anand Kumar

Key Steps

Gather information around customer, product, organization and competition and analyze and plan going forward

Customer Data	Product Data	Organizational Data	Competition
• Who is the customer (segment, trends in terms of customer data, % MS) ? • What are the needs and wants of the customer segment ? • What are the price points which each segment is willing to pay ? • What are the natural partners and preferred distribution channels ? • What is the threat from the buyer ?(buyer power)	• Product USP • Product type (Commodity / niche) • Complementary products in market ? • Any substitute products in market ? • Product stage in life cycle ? • Packaging and delivery models ?	• Company reputation • Special barriers to entry (IP etc ?) • Competence and capabilities analysis ? • Supply chain and distribution models ? • Cost structure • Investment needed • ROI expected • Branding • Financial capabilities	• Market landscape (competitors, market share, market type, CAGR%) • Competitors(MS,products,Su pply chain strategy, branding) • Benchmarks established • Barriers to entry • Supplier power • Other threats • Business risks • Regulatory risks • Deal Killer risks

Typical Use Cases
• Go To Market Strategy and Planning
• Business Strategy

I NEED TO INCREASE MY PROFITS? WHAT DO I NEED TO DO?

If you were asked to study and explore new opportunities to increase revenue, you could explore mergers/acquisitions or also examine developing new products or expanding into new markets. The 7 degrees of freedom framework help in this process.

Overview

This framework is akin to a lateral thinking approach to identify new growth opportunities and is a variant of the Ansoff matrix. This type of approach is most effective when analyzed with associated costs and market conditions.

7 Degrees Of Freedom

Mehrdad Baghai, Stephen Coley and David White

Key Steps

The 7 degrees are :

1.Explore selling existing products to existing customers.
2. Explore acquiring new customers in existing markets.
3. Create new products and services.
4. Developing new value delivery approaches.
5. Moving into new geographies.
6. Analyzing and creating new industry structures.
7. Opening up new competition arenas.

Typical Use Cases

• Sales and marketing strategy
• Business development planning
• Pivoting or course correction of the business
• Strategy planning

I NEED TO TRACK HOW WELL MY BUSINESS IS DOING? HOW DO I DO THAT?

Unwavering focus and alignment are key to success in any initiative. Critical Success Factors helps you to track and measure your progress toward achieving strategic goals. They also provide a reference point which helps everyone align with what is most important, ensuring that tasks and projects are aligned across teams and departments.

Critical Success Factors
Ronald Daniel & John F Rockart

Overview

Critical success factors are those variables or inflection points necessary to enable a positive outcome for a business initiative or strategy. They are also referred to as Key Result Areas (KRA's). Each KRA is associated with a target goal and should be measurable.

Key Steps

Step 1

Industry Level CSF (target goal metric defined and tracked)

Step 2

Environmental CSF resulting from economic or technology changes (target goal metric defined and tracked)

Step 3

Strategy CSF from the business strategy in place (target goal metric defined and tracked)

Step 4

Temporal CSF from internal organizational needs and changes (target goal metric defined and tracked)

Typical Use Cases

- Business Strategy
- Business Planning
- Sales & Marketing Strategy

HOW DO I IMPROVE THE PERFORMANCE OF THE BUSINESS?

You work in an organization making energy metering products and want to increase yield, You could also be part of a team trying to implement culture change in order to improve leadership and workforce capabilities for achieving strategic goals, you could also be building new ways of being efficient and effective in developing software. DMAIC can be used in all these use cases.

Overview

DMAIC is a framework which is primarily used in performance improvement solutions.This framework is used in tactical and strategic projects and is associated with six sigma quality framework and also lean concepts.

DMAIC

Key Steps

- Define the goals (D)
- Measure the performance defining metrics(M)
- Analyze the gap between actual performance and goals defined (A)
- Improve the performance using various tools and techniques (I)
- Control the new system/process (C)

Typical Use Cases

- Complex problem solving
- Performance improvement on a current process

STEPS TO BUILDING VALUE AND COMPETING WITH COMPETITORS

How do you create greater value than the cost of creating something? this is something which can be analyzed by the Porter's value chain framework. You can also analyse how your company creates value and look for ways to add more value thus creating a strong competitive strategy.

Porter's Value Chain
Michael Porter

Overview

This framework is used to create competitive advantage and drive value for your firm by breaking down activities in the firm into primary activities (activities directly related to product) and support activities (activities indirectly associated with product)

Key Steps

Step 1 : Identify primary sub activities.

Step 2: Identify support sub activities.

Step 3 : Identify links between all the value activities we have identified.

Step 4 : look for improving value (value creation-cost of value creation=profit margin).

Typical Use Cases

- Cost optimization
- Value creation
- Increasing Profit Margin

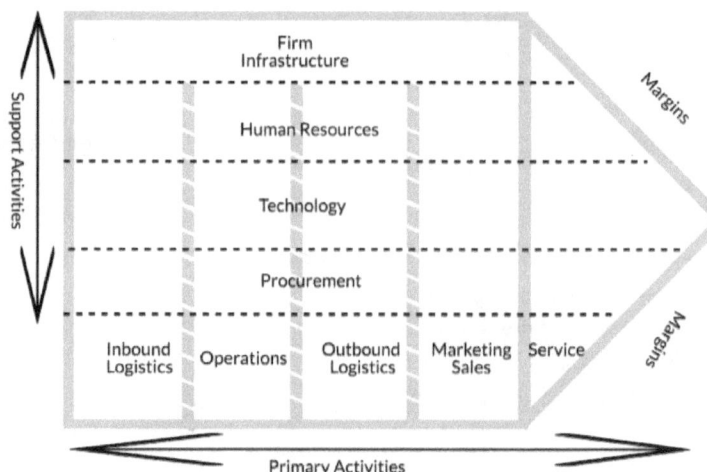

WHAT IS MY MOST VALUABLE MARKET SEGMENT? HOW DO I IDENTIFY IT?

STP (segmentation, targeting and positioning) model is an approach that you can use to identify your most valuable market segments, and then sell to those market segments successfully with carefully positioned and targeted products and marketing.

Overview

The STP model is a customer segmentation model which could be used to identify your most valuable customer segments, and then sell to them using carefully targeted product messaging.

STP Segmentation Model
Kotler and Keller

Key Steps

Step 1 : Segment your marketplace (S).

Step 2 : Target your most attractive customer segment(T).

Step 3 : Position your offering (right product -right marketing message - right customer segment).

Typical Use Cases

- Value selling based on customer segment
- Explore using Pareto's principle along with this model to achieve optimum outcome.
- Customer segmentation and value proposition.

HOW DO I MARKET TO THE RIGHT SET OF CUSTOMERS?

Most marketing campaigns use a "one-size-fits-all" approach, the RFM (Recency, frequency, monetary) model helps you to avoid this approach and helps you to zero onto your most valuable customers.

Overview

The RFM framework is a customer segmentation framework based on the belief that actions of customers in the past predict their future behavior.

Recency/Frequency /Monetary Value

Jan Roelf Bult and Tom Wansbeek

Key Steps

- Recency(R) - How recently did the customer purchase?
- Frequency(F) - How frequently did the customer purchase?
- Monetary Value(M) - How much money did the customer spend ?
- Analyze customer data and stack rank using the RFM factors and segment.

Typical Use Cases

- Customized marketing and targeted marketing
- Tracks customer's preferences over a specific period of time only (watchout)

HOW DO I KNOW THE PREFERRED MARKET FOR MY PRODUCTS?

You have a product and you know your target market includes anyone who has needs but you know that your target market consists of consumers who may have different needs. Customer segmentation provides a framework by dividing your customer base into groups of people(segments) with similar needs. This means that you can meet each segment requirements in a more focused way and fulfil expectations better.

Overview

Customer segmentation is the process of dividing your target market into clearly defined customer subgroups who have common wants, needs and priorities.

Customer Segmentation Model

Kotler And Keller

Key Steps

- Examine your market from a sales perspective.
- Identify prospective customer types.
- Examine commonalities in customer types and then examine segmentation of customer types.
- Segmentation is typically by geography, demography, pyschography or behavioral.
- Ensure that each segment is measurable, substantial in size and viable to be served.

Typical Use Cases

- Sales and marketing strategy
- Product strategy
- Business model
- Strategy planning

HOW DO I KNOW WHAT MY CUSTOMERS VALUE THE MOST?

In the marketplace in which your product operates, value will mean different things to different customers and you need to choose the best way to deliver value to your customers. The Value discipline model helps you with this process.

Overview

This framework is used to develop great value for the customer using the premise that a corporation should specialize in one of three areas - operational excellence , product leadership or customer intimacy. This framework is a variant of Porter's 5 forces.

Value Discipline

Michael Treacy and Fred Wiersema

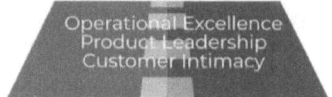

Key Steps

Use the framework outlined below and analyze your organization on customer excellence, operational excellence and product leadership and then plan forward

Operational Excellence Factor - Reliability as core competence, Low cost as core competence, Ease of use, Superior supply chain

Product Leadership Factor - Top of the line product, Cutting edge in terms of product innovation, Strong R & D , Flexible production management

Customer Intimacy Factor - Superior customer service, Customers love the products and the company, Constantly wowing the customer

Typical Use Cases

- Customer Value Proposition Canvas
- Marketing Strategy
- Customer Relationship Management

HOW DO I WOW MY CUSTOMER?

Developing products that exceed customer expectations can be a challenge. Kotler and Keller's 5 product level model helps you understand customer needs and wants and also helps you explore exceeding customer expectations thereby keeping ahead of competitors.

Kotler & Keller's 5 Product Level Model

Kotler – Keller

Overview

This is a framework which helps you analyze and think throgh your various product avatars and correlate it to moving up the value chain in terms of customer expectations. It is helpful in building a product road map.

Key Steps

Step 1 : Typically 5 Product levels :

1. Core benefit
2. Basic product
3. Expected product
4. Augmented product
5. Potential product

Step 2: Analysis of what and how you would like to meet or exceed customer expectations vis-a-vis your product will help you develop a road map.

Typical Use Cases

- Product Strategy Planning
- Structuring product portfolio to target various customer segments
- Go To Market Planning
- Sales and Marketing Strategy

HOW DO I IMPROVE MY CUSTOMER'S EXPERIENCE?

How do your customers experience your business? What do customers experience when they visit your web site or store or use your app? what support do they receive when they buy a product or service? how do they get help when needed? Customer experience mapping helps you map out the ways your customers experience your organization.

Overview

This is a framework which can be used to view your business through your customer's eyes.

Customer Experience Mapping
Ron Zemke and Chip Bell

Key Steps

- Define objective of the mapping exercise - what do you want to be the end result ?
- Gather information.
- Identify touch points of the customer.
- Outline the key stages.
- Start mapping.
- Validate your map.
- Analyze results.

Customer Journey Stages

Discovery/awareness

Research about your product

Purchase product

Delivery of product

After sales support

Review and rate

Share feedback

Typical Use Cases

- Customer relationship management strategy
- Product marketing and sales strategy
- Customer service model

HOW WELL IS MY TEAM ORGANIZED TO DELIVER SUCCESS FOR MY BUSINESS?

You have been asked if the organization is ready to handle the change from traditional operations to a digital model or if there is a significant change management issue in the organization. If this is the case, you can explore using the McKinsey 7S model which helps you in understanding how well your organization is positioned to achieve its goals. You will also be able to get an idea of the elements are key to implement change successfully.

Overview

This model is a framework to help you assess seven critical elements of your business that need to change or be aligned in order for the business to be successful. Each element has an impact on the other as they are interdependent. It is also important to do an AS-IS and a FUTURE state assessment as well.

Key Steps

Analyze each aspect of the project or initiative from a shared goals perspective and study if the interrelationships are healthy or not.

Typical Use Cases

- Organizational Assessment
- Assessing and Tracking key business objectives
- Trace performance problems in an organization to subsequently change and/or improve.
- Mergers & Acquistions

McKinsey 7S

Tom Peters

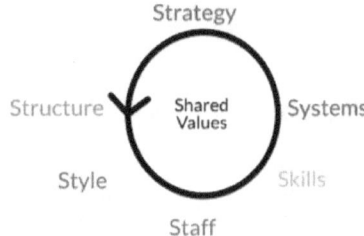

HOW DO I SELF-EVALUATE MY BUSINESS AND SEE WHERE I STAND?

SWOT Analysis is a great framework to use to assess your organization's current position before you decide on any new approach or strategy. It helps you find out what's working well, what's not working out and what does the external world look like from your organizations standpoint.

Overview

SWOT analysis is used to determine how closely a business is aligned with its growth plans and success benchmarks. It can also be used to ascertain how well a particular project is performing according to initial expectations as well.

SWOT Analysis

Key Steps

Strengths	*Weaknesses*
What the business is doing well Resources skills and capabilities Marketplace advantage	What the business lacks or is not doing well Areas of improvement Marketplace disadvantage
Opportunities	*Threats*
What opportunities exist which can benefit the business	What critical issues could put the business at risk

Typical Use Cases

- Business Strategy
- Business Planning
- Project Reviews
- Operational Reviews

HOW DO I KNOW IF I HAVE PLANNED MY RESOURCING RIGHT?

Do you know how many resources you need on your new project? Do you know what resources you have? Capacity planning is an issue of supply and demand and one that can decide how things work out into the future.

Overview

This framework helps you when analyzing resource availability and utilization(increasing capacity, decreasing capacity, acquiring a direct competitor)

Capacity Planning

Key Steps

Step 1 : Analyze Demand - Determine market perspective (CAGR%, market life cycle), Determine company growth (market share %, sentiments, sustainability of growth), Identify and segment demand sources, Analyze growth trends by segment, Use Pareto's principle to identify and understand where the demand is heading.

Step 2 : Analyze Supply - Understand supplier power, Determine industry supply dynamics , Any Opportunities to increase productivity using technology and lower costs ?, Segment industry supply by market segment for analysis

Step 3 : Analyze Expansion opportunity and costs - Does the Company have financial strength to accommodate expansion ?, What is the opportunity cost ? (ROI , payback period, break even), What are the viable alternatives ? (outsourcing, sub lease, lease , OEM partner, sub contract)

Typical Use Cases

- Business Operations Planning
- Capacity management
- Enterprise resource plannin
- Manufacturing resource planning
- Overall equipment effectiveness

I NEED TO BUILD A STRATEGY FOR MY BUSINESS, WHERE DO I START?

If you were asked to develop a strategy for your company, you would most likely decide to get the team together and brainstorm opportunities, and then plan how to take advantage of them. Unfortunately, while this type of approach is important, there is a lot more needed to get it right. We need to look at competitors, culture and capabilities of your organization and see if we can use your company's capabilities to the fullest. This 5P framework helps in that perspective.

Overview

This is an internal looking framework for an organization working on it's strategy and has to be used in conjunction with other external looking frameworks like 4 forces or PESTEL as the challenge with this is that intricacies of industry, market, capabilities and competence are not covered.

5P Strategy

Henry Mintzberg

Key Steps

Follow the steps outlined below and analyze and plan forward

Planning - What are the plans within the organization ?

Ploy - What are the different plans to beat the competition ?

Patterns - Do we have consistent, organized working models ?

Positions - How is our position in the marketplace ?

Perspective - What is our vision ? how is our critical thinking?

Typical Use Cases

- Organizational Analysis
- Strategy Planning

HOW DO I USE MY PRODUCT INNOVATION AND GET AHEAD IN THE MARKET?

The Teece Innovation model is used to help organizations better understand how to capitalize on their innovation and get ahead of the competition. You can use it when you have innovated on something and want to ensure that you capitalize on the innovation and also not lose out to competition.

Overview

This framework is useful to figure out how a business can profit from its own innovation. The framework also indicates that imitability and complementary products will have a strong influence in determining who will ultimately profit from an innovation. The framework suggests that Protecting your idea, finding the dominant design and reaching scale quickly are options.

Innovation Win Lose Model
David Teece

Protect Your Idea

- Can you patent your idea ?
- Can you identify a key supplier and lock them into a binding contract ?
- Venture capitalists would not be interested in investing in businesses whose ideas cannot be protected.

Find The Dominant Design

- Is your design easy to copy or imitate ?
- Can you build your design such that it's not easy to copy ?
- Do you have a strategy for dealing with dominant competitors ?

Scale Quickly

- Can you use lean startups models and build your MVP model, validate and scale ?
- Should you license /partner or build your own channels for scaling quickly ?

Typical Use Cases

- Strategy & Operations Planning
- Product Innovation & Portfolio Management

HOW DO I SOLVE A COMPLEX BUSINESS ISSUE?

You have been assigned a task to solve a festering problem in the organization. The Ishikawa fishbone diagram is a tool that can help you perform a cause and effect analysis for the problem you are trying to solve and discover the root cause of the problem.

Overview

A cause and effect diagram, often called a "Fishbone" diagram, can help in brainstorming to identify possible causes of a problem. It is a visual way to look at cause and effect, the problem or effect is displayed at the head or mouth of the fish and possible causes are the bones of the fish.

Fishbone Diagram

Kaoru Ishikawa

How To Use

1. List problem that has to be studied or analyzed further.
2. The head of the fish is created by listing the problem in a statement format and drawing a box around it.
3. A horizontal arrow is then drawn across the page with an arrow pointing to the head, this acts as the backbone of the fish.
4. Then at least three to four important "causes" are identified that might contribute to the problem (Techniques, skills, equipment, people, materials, environment or measurements).
5. These causes are then drawn to branch off from the spine with arrows, making the first bones of the fish.
6. For each overarching cause, use techniques like the 5 Whys or the 4P's (Policies, Procedures, People and Plant) to identify contributing factors and written down to branch off their corresponding cause.
7. This process of breaking down each cause is continued until the root causes to the problem have been identified. The team then analyzes the diagram until an outcome and next steps are agreed upon.

Typical Use Cases

• Root Cause Analysis

• Problem Solutioning

• Problem definition and
  solving

HOW DO I BUILD AN INNOVATION FOCUSED BUSINESS?

The McKinsey horizons of growth model helps ensure that your organization stays resilient and sustain themselves and avoid the downturn and continue to wow customers with their innovation and creativity by developing new ideas and building an innovation engine replacing older products and businesses as they fall out of favour in the marketplace.

Overview

This framework is about keeping you focused on growth and innovation. This strategy framework requires you to categorize your goals into 3 different 'horizons' (The present core business; the immediate future by extending revenue streams of current business;creating and launching new elements of business that do not exist today). Each Horizon will have a different ROI window and businesses will do well to focus on all 3 stages at same time.

McKinsey 3 Horizons Of Growth
Baghai, Coley, and White

Key Steps

There are 3 horizons to be thought through and for organizations to focus on.

Horizon 1 : This time period is to defend and extend core business which the business is engaged on.

Horizon 2 : This time period is to extend your revenue stream by investing in R&D and nurturing and scaling emerging businesses.

Horizon 3 : This time period focus is on creating options for future businesses. This includes scaling investments, POC's research projects etc.

Typical Use Cases

- Product Portfolio Planning
- Business Strategy
- Future Organizational Roadmap planning

HOW DO I GO ABOUT IMPLEMENTING A DIGITAL TRANSFORMATION PROJECT?

Your organization would like to embark on a digital transformation project. They have asked you to come up with a plan for the same. Digital transformation blueprint is the plan of action you will prepare to help your organization use digital technologies to create new or modify existing business processes, culture and customer experiences.

Digital Transformation Blueprint

Anand Kumar

Overview

Digital transformation is the process of using digital technologies to create new or modify existing business processes, culture, and customer experiences to meet changing business and market requirements. A key part of this is having a digital strategy blueprint planned.

Key Steps

The process towards digital transformation is six steps

Step 1 : Capture the current business strategy (Financial objectives, customer objectives, people objectives and internal process objectives).

Step 2 : Analyze current digital state (Analysis has to be done on Market Forces, Technologies and current systems used, Analyze each departmental function for digital state and finally analyze organization which includes digital readiness, culture etc.).

Step 3 : Design future digital state of organization.

Step 4 : Define the digital transformation program.

Step 5 : Build the financial model ($ needed, ROI etc).

Step 6 : Manage and control the project for successful completion.

Typical Use Cases

- Digitization Projects
- Business Transformation
- Digital Business Models

AM I MAKING THE RIGHT DECISIONS IN MY BUSINESS?

Scenario analysis can be used to bring about some rationality to your decision making and enable you to make the best possible choice. This framework is useful to brainstorm approaches on projects and explore worst and best case.

Scenario Analysis

Herman Kahn

Overview

This is a framework used for building certainty into your decision making on how to deal with a situation. This framework could be used for hypothesis based problem solving approaches. Useful for problem identification and problem definition.

Key Steps

Step 1 - Define the problem and the timeline within which to solve the problem

Step 2 - Identify key trends, factors, uncertainities that may affect plan

Step 3 - Explore using PESTEL analysis if the problem is a longer, complex problem

Step 4 - Stack rank the uncertainties and assumptions with most critical on top

Step 5 - Take top uncertainity/assumption - define good, medium and bad outcomes, analyze and conclude

Typical Use Cases

- Strategic planning
- Business Planning
- Situational Risk Analysis

CAN I PREDICT WHAT MY COMPETITORS MAY DO?

What if you could make close to reality predictions about how competitors will respond to your organizations moves? What if you could use a scientific method to do it? That is what Game theory helps with.

Overview

Game theory is a model where you use reason to predict future behavior and typically applies in situations where a person's success in making choices depends upon choices of others. Typically 2 approaches: Simultaneous move games and Sequential move games.

Game Theory
John von Neumann

Key Steps

a. Simultaneous move games where all players move at same point in time (eg.: companies which launch products at the start of the holiday season or calendar year).
b. Sequential move games where players take turns making moves (eg. : companies competing against each other in launch of products)
c. Build tree diagrams/matrixes/tables and mark potential moves which could be made and using the models and working backwards, strategy could be fine tuned.

Typical Use Cases

- Sales and marketing strategy
- Business modeling
- Strategy planning
- Blue / Red Ocean strategy planning

HOW DO I PLAN FOR COMPETITION?

How did Sony come up with a Walkman which became the rage of that time ? we were happy listening to the vinyl records at home. Later, How did apple come up with the Ipod which became a super success story ? Somehow each company knew that the customer probably wanted something mobile and smaller.

What about introducing shampoos in sachets or cough medicine in plastic pouches ? Many organizations work hard at customer research to find out what their target market wants. But the ones that gain maximum leverage are those that identify wants and needs that we do not even know we have. By challenging deeply held assumptions about their respective industries they are propelled to greatness with minimal competition and redefine the benchmarks for their industry. This is the Blue Ocean strategy model.

Overview

Blue Ocean Strategy helps explore and figure out a market for a product where there is no competition or very less competition. This strategy revolves around searching for a business model in which very few firms operate and where there is no pricing pressure.

Blue Ocean Strategy
W. Chan Kim - Renée Mauborgne

Key Steps

Step 1 : Eliminate: Which factors that the industry has

long competed on should be eliminated?

Step 2 : Reduce: Which factors should be reduced well

below the industry standard?

Step 3 : Raise: Which factors should be raised well above the

industry standard?

Step 4 : Create: Which factors should be created that the

industry has never offered before?

Typical Use Cases

- Business Strategy
- Product Management
- Sales & Marketing Strategy

POINTS TO THINK ABOUT WHEN GROWING MY BUSINESS ABROAD

If your business is planning to expand internationally and you want to minimize the operational risks, the CAGE framework can be used. It can also be used think about how market related factors can affect a business expansion into a new geographical region.

Overview

This a framework which is used to analyze international expansion strategies of your organization. There are Cultural(C), Administrative(A), Geographic(G) and Economic(E) distances which have to be looked at from a cost and time and localization perspective for your expansion to be successful.

CAGE Framework

Pankaj Ghemawat

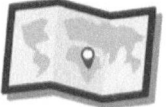

Key Steps

Step 1 : Evaluate **C**ultural distance between your organizational culture at HQ and prevalent culture in the to-be expanded region.
Step 2 : Evaluate **A**dministrative and political distance between your organizational structure and administration at HQ and prevalent structure in the to-be expanded region.
Step 3 : Evaluate **G**eographical distance between your organizational HQ location and the to-be expanded region.
Step 4 : Evaluate **E**conomic distance(GDP, Per capita income etc) between your organizational HQ and the to-be expanded region.

Typical Use Cases

- Sales and marketing strategy
- International expansion planning
- Business modeling for other geographies
- Strategy planning

HOW DO I BUILD MY BUSINESS'S SOCIAL MEDIA PRESENCE?

Social media is now one of the most immediate and powerful ways you can connect with your customers. Social media strategy provides you with a step by step process to ensure you build a good social media presence.

Overview

This framework will help you analyze and build a good social media strategy.You will want to have bi-directional channels with rewards and benefits so that you can a push-pull approach but key is knowing your audience and what content they like in what channel.

Key Steps

- What are your social media goals ?
- What is you current social media status ?
- Do you know what audience you want to cater to?
- Choose the right channel(Pinterest/ Instagram / Facebook/Tic Toc/Telegram/ Twitter or ?)
- Plan your content
- Divide up which channels, when and how often to post
- Plan the social media campaign
- Measure progress based on metrics defined and either persevere or pivot.

Social Media Strategy

Typical Use Cases

- Product launch planning
- Marketing & strategy planning
- Business model building
- Branding& Profile Building

STEPS TOWARDS BUILDING WEB PRESENCE FOR MY BUSINESS

If you have been handed a large web project and the project is to update the web presence and the online store of your organization, you would start by exploring the use of the 4S web marketing framework which is specifically focused on online web marketing.

Overview

This is a framework which can be used to create a holistic approach towards your online business and can be used to create online marketing campaigns, designing and redesigning online marketing models etc.

4 S Web Marketing

Efthymios Constantindes

Key Steps

- **SCOPE** : What is the scope of what you want to ? What is the market potential ? who are the customers ? what is the strategic role of the web site and the web ?
- **SITE:** Is the web site customer focused ? The web site is the core of the campaign. What are customers going to find on your site? Is what they find going to match up with what they were looking for when they clicked on your ad or link? Are they going to come back time after time to make additional purchases or take other actions?
- **SYNERGY** : Is your offline strategy aligned with your online strategy ? focus on front office, back office, 3rd party integration and other areas.
- **SYSTEM** :Making sure your IT system is uptodate with hardware, software etc.

Typical Use Cases

- Online Marketing Campaigns

HOW DO I FIND OUT WHAT MY COMPETITORS ARE DOING?

When you look around at your current competitors, do you know what they are doing? Do you know how effective their current operations are, or how satisfied their customers are? When you develop your business strategies, do you consider what your competitors strategies might be? Do you know review their pricing strategy ? The Competitor assessment model helps you assess your competitor using a structured approach.

Overview

This framework is used to assess your competitor in the marketplace by using a structured objective driven approach.

Competitor Assessment
Michael Porter

Key Steps

Step 1 : What To Assess ?

Strategy : Assess competitor strategy

Operations : What is competitor doing now ?

Customer Perspective : How do customers view the competitor ?

Strengths & Capabilities : What are competitor capabilities now and into the future ? what advantages ?

Market Prospects : What is the current market and how is the competitor positioned ?

Step 2 : How To Assess

Step 1 : **Plan** - What, Why, What is already known?, What will it cost ?, What will you do with the analysis ?

Step2 :**Collect** - Where to look, Who will look, what software will you use , are there any ethical or legal issues ?

Step 3 : **Analyze** - Determine how information collected will be used, what can make your company do better?, how will your competitor react to market trend and what will be their moves ?

Typical Use Cases

- Customer Relationship Management
- Sales & Marketing Strategy
- Business planning & strategy

HOW DO I KNOW THAT ALL PARTS OF MY BUSINESS ARE WORKING WELL TOGETHER?

Congruence model is used to analyse and ensure that all the drivers of your business are aligned. When the drivers of your performance do not work well together, success suffers.

Overview

This framework is primarily used for identifying root causes of performance issues. The framework uses four critical elements - Work, People, Organizational Structure and Organizational culture and suggests that critical analysis of these elements along with analysis of their inter-relatioships may help address the problem.

Congruence Model

Nadler-Tushman

Key Steps

Step 1 : Analyze each element (Type of work, People and capabilities, organizational structure and relationships and culture) in detail

Step 2 : Analyze the relationships between the elements

Step 3 : Identify potential causes and analyze in detail and identify root cause

Step 4 : Build and sustain congruence between the elements

Typical Use Cases

- Performance Management
- Organizational Assessment
- Performance Improvement

IS MY BUSINESS GROWING FROM A HOLISTIC STANDPOINT?

Businesses are organic in nature, they are born, they grow, they enter a prime state and then eventually they decline and die. The corporate lifecycle model helps you guide your business to the prime state and possibly avoid the problems that lead to decline.

Overview

This framework is a self introspection framework and helps alert to signs that the organization is not in optimal state, it also helps do an internal analysis to identify organization's current state.

Corporate Lifecycle
Ichak Adizes

Key Steps

Step 1 : Analyze your organization state currently
Step 2 : Review in context of the lifecycle framework

Typical Use Cases

- Business planning
- Organizational Development

Courtship Stage	Infancy Stage	Go-Go Stage	Adolescence Stage	Prime Stage
Startup idea/team	Sales/Revenue Focus	Conflict	Stable organization	Structured

Signs Of Aging	Aristocracy	Recrimination	Bureacracy	Death
Complacency	Red tape/nepotism	Blame Culture	Rules/process	Die

HOW DO I COMPARE COSTS VS. THE BENEFITS THE BUSINESS MAY GET?

Your boss has assigned a new project to you and you find that your people are struggling to keep up with the increased workload. Hiring resources will cost money but you also need to see if the benefits will outweigh the costs. This is where the cost benefit model will help you.

Overview

This is a framework which can be used to brainstorm cost vs. benefits for primarily non-critical/complex financial decisions.

Cost Benefit Analysis

Key Steps

- Brainstorm cost and benefits for a decision.
- Assign a monetary value to the costs of the decision.
- Assign the monetary value to the benefits of that decision.
- Compare costs and benefits and make the decision to move forward or not.

Typical Use Cases

- Examining investment opportunities on a project
- Analyzing pros and cons
- Analyzing costs from a cost of mitigation, costs of risks, costs of acquisition and implementation while analyzing benefits from a process change or a learning perspective or a context specific benefit perspective.

HOW DO I MAKE A CRITICAL BUSINESS DECISION?

Decision trees provide a visually effective way to lay out options and investigate the possible outcomes of choosing those options. They also help you to form a balanced picture of the risks and rewards associated with each possible course of action. Typically, you start a decision tree with a decision that you need to make and work your way through options and outcomes.

Overview

This is a decision making tool which helps you explore all possible options to solve a problem and analyze each option to determine best outcome. The decision to be made is typically broken down into solution options and each solution option is broken down into outcome options. Assigning probability ratios to each outcome option will help you choose the best probable outcome.

Key Steps

- Start with the decision to be made.
- Break down the decision to be made into various solution options.
- Break down various solution options into outcome options.
- Assign probability ratios to outcome (Try to use pareto's principle).
- Choose the best probable option

Typical Use Cases

- Complex problem solving
- Complex decision making

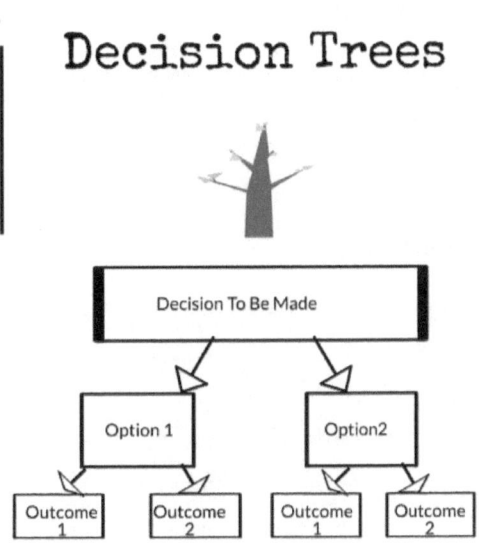

Decision Trees

Decision To Be Made

Option 1   Option2

Outcome 1   Outcome 2   Outcome 1   Outcome 2

HOW DO I KNOW IF I AM DELIVERING WHAT MY BUSINESS NEEDS TO DELIVER?

Gap analysis is a useful technique that enables you to identify the gap between your current state and the future state that you want to be in, along with the tasks that you need to complete to close this gap. This is particularly useful when starting a project.

Overview

Gap analysis is a technique that compares the current state or goals with an ideal state or goals, and highlights shortcomings vis-a-vis the intended goals, The shortcomings can then be used as opportunities for improvement.

Gap Analysis

Key Steps

Step 1 : Identify the area to be analyzed and identify the

objectives to be achieved.

Step 2 : Envision the ideal future state.

Step 3 : Analyze the current state.

Step 4 : Compare the current state with the ideal state.

Step 5 : Describe the gap and quantify the difference.

Step 6 : Create plan to bridge the gap and

summarize recommendations.

Typical Use Cases

- Prioritization and business planning
- Identifying points of failure on a project
- Identifying best areas to deploy resources and focus

I HAVE SO MANY ISSUES TO HANDLE, HOW DO I FOCUS ON THE IMPORTANT ONES?

How do you focus your attention on fixing the most important problems? How do you decide which problems you need to deal with first? . Pareto Analysis helps prioritize possible outcomes by identifying the problems that will be resolved by achieving these outcomes.

Overview

This is a framework which can be used to analyze cause and effects. Pareto's principle states that 80% of the effects could be due to 20% of the causes asserting an unequal relationship between inputs and outputs.

Pareto's Principle
Alfred Pareto

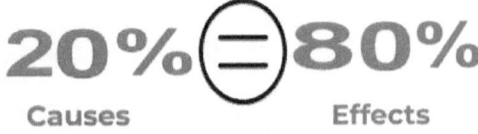

20% ⊜ 80%

Causes   Effects

Key Steps

- Identify and list all problems with a process or an issue.
- Identify the root cause of the problem.
- Assign a score to each problem.
- Group problems by root cause.
- Add up the scores for each group.
- Examine for unequal relationship between causes and effects.

Typical Use Cases

- Quality control
- Sales Planning
- Business development
- Many use cases where problems or issues need to be resolved, Pareto's helps in identification of unequal relationships between inputs and outputs

I NEED TO UNDERSTAND WHY I AM LOSING MONEY IN MY BUSINESS?

When you have to do an analysis to determine why profits are sliding and why your organization is making a loss, problem isolation using profitability analysis framework will help you analyse and help identify factors and help in resolving the issue.

Overview

Using this approach called **PROBLEM ISOLATION**, we can drill down into analyzing profitability and identifying where the problems are. The approach requires you to drill down into good level of detail for further analysis.

Profitability Analysis Framework

Profits

Revenue ← → Cost

Typical Use Cases

- Financial Analysis
- Business Operations Review
- Business Strategy

Revenue /Unit   #Units Sold

Cost/Unit   #Units Sold

Break down revenues or units sold by product/product line; by distribution channel; by region; by customer segment; by industry etc and drill down until you have all the details for analysis. Once you understand what caused the problem, then you can focus on fixing it

Fixed Costs   Variable Costs

Break down fixed and variable costs down into costs by function or use value chain analysis and identify the problem. Once you understand what caused the problem, then you can focus on fixing it

Profits can be generated by increasing revenue or decreasing costs. Isolating the problem and analyzing is key before implementation

WHAT SHOULD I DO TO CREATE THE FUTURE ROAD MAP OF MY BUSINESS?

The first step in any process improvement initiative is to find out exactly where you are as of today. You can then create a future roadmap of where you want to be and compare this to your earlier state and demonstrate improvement.

Overview

This framework summarizes the inputs and outputs of one or more processes in tabular form. It is an acronym that stands for **S**upplies, **I**nputs, **P**rocess, **O**utputs and **C**ustomers and helps in understanding the implications of a process and provides an AS-IS state of a process.

SIPOC

(suppliers, inputs, process, outputs, customers)

Key Steps

Step 1

List Suppliers

Step 2

Determine Inputs

Step 3

List Major elements of Process

Step 4

Identify Outputs

Step5

Define Customers

Typical Use Cases

- Business process reengineering
- Process Mapping
- Ideation
- Business planning

HOW DO I IDENTIFY MY BUSINESS'S BIGGEST BOTTLENECK?

The theory of constraints framework helps identify the most important bottleneck in your processes and systems in your organization which can then be dealt with to improve performance. It is also about strengthening your weakest link.

Overview

This framework is used to the explore the boundary of the problem and identify the constraint and work towards strengthening the weakest link. You would typically use a combination of divergent and convergent thinking.

Theory Of Constraints

Eliyahu M. Goldratt

Key Steps

- Extensively studying and analyzing the process used and identifying the constraint. This involves divergent thinking where all options are explored and noted.
- Exploring different options to exploit the constraint. This involves convergent thinking where options which can best address the constraint are evaluated. I recommend using Pareto's principle here and hypothesis based problem solving as well.
- Subordinate everything else to the constraint.
- Elevate the constraint by the fixes you apply.
- Analyze and evaluate how the constraint is performing with the fixes in place.

Typical Use Cases

- Problem solving especially in manufacturing.
- Identifying the constraint makes it easier to find what is slowing the advancement of the business.
- Constraints focus improvements on where they can have the most impact on profit.
- Provides a structure for continuing improvements.

Anand Kumar - https://www.linkedin.com/in/anandkumarpadmanaban

ABOUT THE AUTHOR

Anand Kumar is a licensed certified manager(CM) from ICPM USA and is a senior professional with over 25 years of experience in High Technology and Professional Services businesses. He is currently business mentor and coach to several start-ups and venture capital firms including Faster Capital, Utilis Capital and also is actively involved in a portfolio of companies in the medical technologies areas as a founder advisor where his primary focus is on driving growth and performance improvement through business, value and developing sustained innovation capability. Anand's expertise is in the areas of New Ventures, Business Model and Value Innovation, the effective use of technology/IT, Business Transformation and Professional Services Business Management.

Anand has been responsible for establishing and growing Information Technology and Knowledge Management Practices in various Fortune 500 companies, such as GD Searle, Pharmacia and Monsanto. Anand has managed international technology transfer and collaboration agreements with companies in Europe and the US. Anand holds a Bachelor's degree in Electronics Engineering, a Master's in Industrial Engineering and a Diploma In Business Administration. Anand also is a trustee with the NGO's People's Education Society and WasteImpact where he advises on rural employability and waste management respectively . During his free time, Anand loves to write, coach and mentor and enjoys watching ideas take shape and deliver successful outcomes. He can be reached at azkuma@gmail.com.

Anand's other book includes "All It Takes Is a Minute" which is a Self-Help book on the nuances of what constitutes a successful person.

www.ingramcontent.com/pod-product-compliance
Lightning Source LLC
Chambersburg PA
CBHW020620220526
45463CB00006B/2633